First published 2021 by Nurturing Brain Potential Pty Ltd

Produced by Independent Ink
independentink.com.au

Copyright © 2021 by Dr Robert Melillo and Dr Genevieve Dharamaraj – all rights reserved

Ollie the Octopus and His Magnificent Brain™ is a trademark registered by Nurturing Brain Potential Pty Ltd
The Melillo Method™ is a trademark registered by Dr Robert Melillo

Apart from any fair dealing for the purposes of study, research or review, as permitted under the *Australian Copyright Act 1968*, no part of this book may be reproduced by any process without written permission of the authors.

This is a work of fiction. Names, places, characters and happenings herein are used fictitiously, or are a product of the authors' imaginations. Dr Robert Melillo, Dr Brandon Crawford, and Dr Kyle Daigle are real people, and their names and likenesses have been used with permission.

Cover image and internal illustrations by Kat Smirnoff
Internal design by Independent Ink
Typeset by Post Pre-press Group, Brisbane

ISBN 978-0-6452957-0-2 (paperback)
ISBN 978-0-6452957-1-9 (epub)
ISBN 978-0-6452957-2-6 (hardcover)

Disclaimer: The content of this book is for informational purposes only and is not intended to diagnose, treat, cure, or prevent any condition or disease. This book does not replace professional therapeutic evaluation of a child's development, and use of the retained reflexes integration should not occur without supervision from a qualified health care practitioner. Please consult with your child's physician or health care practitioner regarding suggestions made in this book. Any liability arising from unauthorised and/or unsupervised use of this book and the techniques herein is excluded to the maximum extent permissible. The use of this book implies your acceptance of this disclaimer.

OLLIE THE OCTOPUS
and His Magnificent Brain™

The Melillo Method™ and Integrating Primitive Reflexes

Dr Robert Melillo (Chiropractor, USA) and
Dr Genevieve Dharamaraj (Chiropractor)
Illustrated by Kat Smirnoff

This book is dedicated to:

All the kids who have developmental delay or glitches in the brain. May you know hope, and take comfort in the fact that the brain is neuroplastic and with the Melillo Method™, your true potential will shine.

To my son Ryan, know that there is no limit to your potential and you are my reason why.

To my husband Richard, thanks for the support and faith in my crazy ventures.

To my mentor Dr Robert Melillo, who has spent his lifetime working on the Melillo Method™ to change the lives of so many children and adults who have a disconnected brain. I am eternally grateful to your generous gift in allowing me to shine the light for your work in Australia.

To my mentors Dr Kyle Daigle and Dr Brandon Crawford, thank you for being powerhouses in functional neurology, for designing tools that enhance the Melillo Method™ and changing lives around the world. I'm so grateful to call you my friends.

To my co-pilots Adele Raj-Manning and Chris Manning, for editing and adding some creative language to my story, and for your belief in my dreams.

To my amazing team at Nurturing Brain Potential, touching and changing lives every day. Karen, my amazing wingman who helped set up NBP; Caz, who keeps NBP running; and the fabulous Sophie, Ashley, Frank, Maddi, Amelia, Caleb and Zoe, who go above and beyond to ensure each client reaches their true potential.

To Ann, my publisher who supported and had faith in getting this book to print.

To the talented Kat, our illustrator who breathed life into Ollie.

Foreword by Dr Robert Melillo

The most important challenge that we face today is the unprecedented rise of neurobehavioural disorders in children. The most significant reasons are primarily environmental and lifestyle. The same factors that have caused a dramatic rise in issues such as obesity, diabetes, and heart disease in adults are the same we see in kids around the world.

The most important tools to combat these rising issues are education and awareness. Dr Genevieve Dharamaraj does a wonderful job of educating children about a wide variety of issues in a fun and entertaining way. She gives the solutions to these issues and most importantly gives them hope. We can accept a person's differences and challenges, but we mustn't blindly accept their disability and sit back and allow them to struggle and suffer.

In most children, their strengths outweigh their weaknesses. In kids with learning and behavioural issues these weaknesses overwhelm their natural strengths and result in struggles to do basic things. It is important that they understand that these problems are not because they are weak or unintelligent. There is nothing "wrong" with them; they are not broken. We have to teach them that sometimes during development certain imbalances can develop, making it hard for them to do certain things. However, this developmental imbalance can be improved and often completely corrected.

Some children are born with certain areas on one side of the brain that are more strongly connected than others; they are actually gifted. They have areas on one side of the brain that are unusually strong and overwhelm the weaker or underdeveloped areas. Either side of this imbalance produces symptoms and challenges. In Attention Deficit Hyperactive Disorder (ADHD) the deficit is in the networks on the right side of the brain that control attention. The hyperactivity comes from overactive networks on the left hemisphere of the brain. This results in overactive movement, impulsivity, and emotional outburst. Kids with ADHD are also known to be highly intelligent and have exceptional skills which are almost always connected to left hemisphere functions. A child may be an early word reader and later struggle in reading comprehension. This can seem confusing unless you look at it in the light of the brain hemispheres. The left brain controls word reading; the right brain, reading comprehension. This is also true with mathematical skills, with one side of the brain controlling memorisation and the other, comprehension.

Once this imbalance develops, it will not self-correct and will have an impact throughout life. Many will learn to compensate for their weaknesses and there are doctors, therapists and teachers who will help them try to improve and manage these issues. However, most families and children who have these imbalances are told that there is nothing that can be done to improve these challenges. They are told to "just accept it" and not hope for change. This can be devastating to both the parents and the kids. Because there is no physical damage in the brain, no genetic mutations, no broken genes, the brain can be properly stimulated and therefore balanced.

The concept of neuroplasticity that has developed over the past several decades has shown us that the brain can change in much more profound ways than we ever dreamed of before. The brain is like a muscle and with proper use and stimulation any area of the brain and its functions can improve, especially when there is no physical damage or defect. It is so important to empower these children and their families.

Restoring hope through education and storytelling is what I believe is the most brilliant accomplishment of the author. I am so excited to be a part of this book! I am humbled and honoured that Dr Genevieve Dharamaraj has taken my work and written this beautiful, entertaining, and empowering story for children and families with such a positive message. I highly recommend that all children read this book to understand and help each other overcome these challenges while understanding, respecting and accepting each other's differences.

Chapter One: Ollie the Octopus and His Magnificent Brain™

Deep, deep down, miles below the wild whitecaps that surround the eastern shore of Tasmania, lays another world. Sea creatures of all colours, shapes and sizes live amongst the huge blades of the giant brown kelp forest. One of them is Ollie the Octopus.

Ollie is trying to juggle the shiny seashells sitting on the sea floor. Oops! Just when he picks up a seashell with one of his tentacles, he drops another. He is one big giant clumsy butterfingers!

"Argh!"

In frustration, Ollie decides to whirl. Round, and round, and round he goes, just using one of his good tentacles, whirling on the seabed and creating a plume of sand and rocks that goes hurtling in every direction.

Bang! Boom! Crash!

All the other sea creatures dart and scurry as far away as possible from Ollie.

It is not long before Ollie's mum sees the cloud of sand and hears the hullabaloo. Oh no, is that one of Ollie's *tantrums* again?

When Ollie has a tantrum, Ollie's mum feels a mix of emotions. She turns the deepest shade of purple, a sign of a terribly embarrassed octopus. Ollie's mum does love him very much. Her heart feels so very heavy because she knows that Ollie is hurting.

"Ollie, stop that!" she cries.

Ollie slinks over. This isn't the first time that he has been in trouble.

"Please sit quietly beside me," she says.

Ollie sits on the rock shelf, but within seconds he starts to squirm and begins tapping. He is a Mr Fidgety Boots! He just cannot stay still, no matter how hard he tries.

Dr Robert Melillo

Huge waves are crashing on the surface, creating ripples that travel deep down to the seabed, pulling and pushing the kelp forest this way and that.

Ollie is playing by himself, weaving in and out of the dancing kelp. He spies a diver and he can't decide if he should stay or if he should swim away in a puff of black ink. Ollie by nature is a curious creature, so he decides to stay. He grabs some kelp leaves and wraps them all around himself, with only one beady eye peeping out.

Dr Robert Melillo, world-renowned scuba diver, professor, best-selling author of *Disconnected Kids*, researcher and clinician, has decided to visit the beautiful kelp forest.

Ollie is a little shy, so he stays camouflaged.

A week passes and Dr Robert comes to visit the kelp forest again.

This time Ollie is feeling brave and courageous, so he swims up to Dr Robert.

"Hi, I'm Ollie. What's your name?" Ollie says.

"Hi, my friends call me Dr Rob."

Dr Rob notices that one of Ollie's tentacle is misbehaving.

Dr Rob says, "Ollie, I think you may be having issues with your tentacle due to *functional disconnection*. It's a big word that means you may have a glitch in your brain where the messages are not being received or transmitted, so it is a faulty messaging system." Dr Rob explains further that this could be causing Ollie's fidgeting and his clumsy ways.

Dr Rob continues, explaining to Ollie that his brain is *neuroplastic*. Wow, another big word! It means the brain can always improve. The Melillo Method™, designed by Dr Robert Melillo, is a way to help Ollie's brain be truly magnificent. It's about removing the glitches and getting the brain to fire properly. There could be some exercises for Ollie to help integrate primitive reflexes.

"Dr Rob, Dr Rob, you mean I can really have a magnificent brain without glitches?" Ollie is so excited his tentacles are flying in all directions. "Can we have a Melillo party in the kelp forest? Please say yes! I will bring my mum and all my friends. I can't wait to tell them I can have a magnificent brain!"

Did you know that when you are born your brain weighs 400g, the same as 4 apples? And by the time you are an adult, it weighs 1.4kg - the same as 14 apples! Your brain needs fuel and activation to grow. When you go from a baby to a toddler, the brain has a massive GROWTH EXPLOSION. There is a correct order that the brain needs to grow, or there could be glitches just like Ollie has.

There are reflexes called "primitive reflexes" that are there to help you when you are born, and when you are learning to crawl and walk. They should disappear in a certain order, by certain ages, so that your brain can grow with new skills. If they don't go away, then your brain may have these "glitches" that can create some problems, like the ones Ollie has or with things like learning at school.

Chapter Two:
The Melillo Party in the Kelp Forest

It is finally the day of the party and there is a buzz of excitement amongst all the sea creatures in the kelp forest. Ollie's mum, however, is in despair as Ollie was up at a ridiculous hour, well before the rays of dappled sunlight filtered through the forest.

"It's today! It's today, it's today!" Ollie screams, giving his mum a massive headache.

Suddenly, the shadows of three divers appear as the sea creatures wait eagerly deep below the surface. It is Dr Robert with two other master divers. Dr Rob introduces them to the group as Dr Kyle Daigle, the inventor of some really cool video games that can help the brain, and Dr Brandon Crawford, an expert on the use of his amazing laser on the brain. They are the three Neuro Musketeers and are famous all around the world.

Have you ever wondered about how the brain develops from mushy baby brain to the incredible beings we are?

Do you know that there are two sides to the brain? You got it, a right and left brain connected in the middle. By having two sides, we can do more as each side of the brain develops special skills.

The first three years of life are spent growing connections in our right brain. It is so important that we have no interruptions to this as it could cause glitches. The right brain is about the big picture, and the left brain becomes our radar for details.

Ollie and his friends gather around in awe.

The party is in full swing! The sensational Southern Oceanic Orchestra is playing sea music, an odd mixture of bubbles, drumming and swishes in the water. It's a rare treat and some of the sea creatures are dancing wildly to these tunes. Others are participating in various different games. Delicious morsels are being offered to all, carried on large trays by very dapper blacktip reef sharks, who weave amongst the creatures.

I'm not sure that Dr Rob or his friends, Dr Kyle and Dr Brandon, are eating anything though. I think they have a very different palate to what is on offer!

It's time for Ollie to get checked. He is so excited that he knocks Dr Rob to the ground and needs Dr Kyle to calm him down.

The Melillo Method™ exam begins!

Dr Rob reports that the reason Ollie's behaviour is so erratic, and why he has meltdowns and avoids eye contact, is due to his right brain not developing as it should have. Dr Rob reassures Ollie's mum that it was not her fault, and there are many, many reasons for this to occur. Ollie was in such a rush to grow up that he may have missed a couple of steps in development. He ran before he could walk, as they say.

Primitive reflexes are designed to help us. Some of them start while we are still in the womb, and some are developed after we are born. They are like training wheels for our brain. Have you tried riding a bicycle with training wheels? They are great when you are first learning how to ride but they can really slow you down when you have already mastered bike riding. Imagine if you grow your brain with training wheels attached. You can never ride fast or do super cool tricks. This is what happens when we still have primitive reflexes when we have grown up. It makes it harder at school with certain learning skills. The primitive reflexes we needed as a baby should have almost disappeared by the time we are a toddler. If they don't disappear, there could be glitches in our brain. The age we first crawl or the timing of our first steps tells us how our brain is doing.

Dr Kyle checks out Ollie's primitive reflexes. He has quite a few retained reflexes, and that explains a lot about Ollie's behaviour. The startle reflex, or Moro reflex, explains the meltdowns that Ollie often experiences, plus that sick-in-the-tummy feeling Ollie always has that makes him feel a little "cray-cray".

The Melillo Method™ is the result of a lifetime of work by Dr Robert Melillo. It is so exciting that even Harvard Medical School did some research on it, with fabulous results. Dr Rob explains that Ollie has to do some exercises that will help his right brain develop more connections. It is because the brain is neuroplastic and LOVES learning new things. No matter how old you are.

Ollie says excitedly, "Does that mean I can truly become the best octopus juggler in the Seven Seas?"

Dr Rob replies, "Ollie, your brain can truly be magnificent!"

Chapter Three: Stormy the Starfish

Stormy the Starfish is a beautiful creature with five brilliantly coloured orange arms. Did you know that a starfish is not actually a fish? Isn't that strange! That is why scientists prefer to call these lovely animals "sea stars".

Stormy's name, however, is a very fitting name for her. Stormy has a quick temper and can get terribly angry over the smallest thing and isn't afraid to show it. When Stormy stomps past, the other creatures sneak away and murmur, "Here comes Stormy, there is about to be a storm in a teacup." It is such a shame, as Stormy actually wants to have friends to play with. Despite her bluster, she is terribly anxious and very lonely.

Stormy is the next patient on the list. Dr Brandon lowers his hand to the seabed and Stormy slides onto his outstretched palm. Dr Brandon carefully conducts the primitive reflex check and finds that Stormy has the retained startle reflex. This could explain the conundrum that is Stormy. Sometimes this reflex makes you hyperactive or causes problems with your memory. As the entire neighbourhood of the kelp forest knows, Stormy never remembers anyone's name.

Before the party started, Ollie secretly told Dr Brandon that he found Stormy a little difficult to be friends with. He is even a little scared of her, ever since that day a few months ago when Stormy lashed out and hit Ollie in the head with her strong two arms. As always with Stormy, it was a to-do over nothing. Ollie had just picked up a cowrie shell and, in his clumsy way, had accidently bumped her off her perch on the rock. It was just a gentle nudge. The hit on his head from Stormy was definitely not a nudge! Ollie thinks he still has a mark on his head to prove it.

Dr Brandon demonstrates the starfish exercises that Stormy has to do. As Stormy is practicing these exercises, Dr Brandon whispers to Ollie that Stormy will be less stormy if she does all her exercises. Ollie's tentacles start twitching with excitement. He would really like to be friends with Stormy. He can't wait for Stormy to shine like a star.

The startle reflex, or Moro reflex, refers to the reaction a baby has to a loud noise or sudden moment where their arms and legs shoot out like a starfish. This reflex is also the earliest development of the "fight or flight" instinct. Babies are born in this state, and it is only after the first year of life that the vagal system, or calming system, develops. The vagal system enables a baby to soothe themselves to sleep.

The fight or flight instinct describes how you react when in danger. So, if you happen to be swimming and see a shark, your heart will start to race and you will breathe heavily. Your brain decides if you should swim away fast, or stay and punch the shark in the nose! What do you think you would do?

Chapter Four: Silly Sally the Shrimp

Every year, the kelp forest has an athletic carnival. It is usually a day of anticipation and excitement except for one of Ollie's closest friends. Sally the Shrimp dreads the day when it comes around, often pleading with a tummy ache as an excuse to not be in the race. She gets teased mercilessly about her running style. It has to be seen to be believed, as it is truly comical and, frankly, looks plain silly. Can you imagine running in REALLY high heels? That's the way Sally runs. She often topples over, usually causing a pile-up on the ocean floor. It is particularly upsetting for Sally because, you see, Sally was named after the Sally Lightfoot crab! Sally Lightfoot crabs are the fastest runners in all of the oceans.

Everyone on race day usually gives Sally a wide berth as they have all experienced being on the bottom of the pile-up. Being squished by all the sea creatures is not a fun way to spend the athletic carnival. The first aid officer often has quite a hectic time pulling everyone off the ocean bed and checking for injuries.

Sally is also on Dr Rob's patient list. Dr Rob's examination finds that Sally has a retained primitive reflex called the Babinski reflex. He explains that this is due to developmental delay. Sally's brain never quite got the right foundations to build up a smooth running style. It was because Sally was in such a hurry to run before she crawled properly that the brain developed this glitch. To be able to walk and run properly, the Babinski reflex needs to disappear at a certain stage in development. Dr Rob recommends some easy exercises that Sally needs to do twice a day.

Ollie is very excited for his bestie, Sally. It is just as well the athletic carnival is just around the corner. For the first time in her life, Sally actually has a chance at the trophy. Never in her wildest dreams did Sally think she would have a shot at winning in a running race. The night before the athletic carnival, Sally dreams of running like her namesake creatures, leaping, jumping and seemingly flying past all the other competitors. A trophy is definitely within her reach.

Chapter Five: Daisy the Dyslexic Dolphin

Ollie is most concerned about one of his friends, Daisy the Dolphin. Daisy often appears to be happy and carefree to others but, being one of her best friends, Ollie knows that Daisy has a secret. Daisy's deepest and darkest secret makes her feel so small and very ashamed. Octopuses and dolphins are some of the most intelligent sea creatures. So, there were signs that Ollie recognised that meant things just didn't add up!

Daisy is an absolute champion at sports, excelling in gymnastics with moves that you could not possibly imagine, surfing the most gigantic waves with super fantastic acrobatics that are met with gasps of awe and shivers. No one could imagine that Daisy is hiding a shameful and embarrassing secret. It is her Achilles heel, and it bubbles underneath the surface, darkening the most beautiful of days.

How could the most intelligent of sea creatures admit that she struggles with reading? Even the most basic of books, the simplest books that the sea creatures in kindergarten could rattle off. The pressure of being an intelligent creature but not being able to read torments Daisy, as she often gets teased and bullied. Poor Daisy is made to feel dumb, so she hides her feelings by being a clown in class, drawing attention away from her secret.

When Daisy attempts to read, the words on the page seem to run and disappear, as if they were written in ink and water was poured on them. It is a jumble of lines and it just makes no sense to Daisy's brain. How do words come from that? Daisy often wondered!

Ollie really wants Daisy to be checked by Dr Rob. Daisy, however, is in awe of him, and a little intimidated. Ollie persuades Daisy to get checked by Dr Kyle instead. Using the Melillo Method™, Dr Kyle explains to Daisy that her left brain shows signs of developmental delay, and her struggles are due to her left brain not being able to process the meaning of words like it should. This delay makes reading incredibly difficult and it is no sign of her intelligence. The brain can be stimulated to produce better processing, and if Daisy does the exercise, her brain will fire up the networks needed for her to read better.

Daisy beams with this news and can't contain her excitement! She races off and torpedoes into a breaking wave before performing a triple somersault with a twist. Dr Kyle's face lights up as this is truly his life passion, unleashing potential with the Melillo Method™.

Chapter Six: Chaotic Cary the Crab

A week before the Melillo party . . .

On a dull and dismal day, Ollie spies Chaotic Cary sitting in the doldrums with his notebook open and just sighing. Ollie races up to him, creating his usual swirls and little clouds of sand storms. Cary gazes at Ollie and lets out the biggest sigh.

"What's up?" Ollie cries whilst swimming furiously around Cary. Ollie tries to read Cary's notebook, but can't make any sense of the scribbles and odd marks that fill the page.

"Are you writing in a secret code?" asks Ollie. "Oh, I know! You are writing in *hieroglyphics*," says Ollie with a smug smile. It's such a big word that Ollie has just learnt earlier today in his history class, when his teacher explained the writing of the Ancient Egyptians on pyramid walls.

Cary scowls, "Of course not! Can't you read?"

"Sorry!" says Ollie, remembering a little too late that Cary has the reputation of having the messiest handwriting anyone has ever seen.

"I can't do this homework," Cary whines. "It's too hard!"

Crabs communicate by waving their pincers, and Cary has the reddest, shiniest pair of pincers in the whole kelp forest, but when he tries to write it's like they have a mind of their own. It's as if aliens have taken control over Cary's pincers and all he has to show for his efforts is a big huge scrawly mess on the page.

Cary lets out yet another big sigh that shakes his whole body, picks up his books and, in a sideways dance, scoots off to the distant corner of the kelp forest.

Ollie slumps on the seabed as another potential friend slinks away.

On the day of the Melillo party . . .

The party is in full swing. Cary has been hiding, partly buried in sand at the very edges of the gathering. His black beady eyes pop out of his bright orange shell, scanning the queues that have formed for the assessments by Dr Melillo, Dr Rob and Dr Kyle. His eyes pop back into his shell and he burrows deeper into the sand.

The shifting sand catches Ollie's attention and he sees just a tiny fleck of Cary's bright shell. Ollie recalls the last encounter he had with Cary a week ago. Ever since he started doing his exercises, Ollie has turned into a positive, "can do" octopus. Ollie races off to grab Dr Kyle and begs him to check Cary.

Dr Kyle is an obliging and kind-hearted individual. He swims over and coaxes Cary out of his hole. Dr Kyle gently examines Cary and ignores his sighs and huffs. After all, he is used to working with kids.

"Cary, I think you have dysgraphia. This is because you have the palmer primitive reflex," explains Dr Kyle.

"What??? Dissy graaapia?"

"Dysgraphia is an impairment which causes poor or untidy writing. It is a sign of a left-brain imbalance, and kids are generally clumsy when working with their hands. The palmer reflex is a primitive reflex also known as the grasp reflex. It's when a baby grabs your finger and doesn't let go. It should have gone by four to six months. Cary, you still have this reflex which makes it difficult to use a pencil or pen."

Cary's shell gets brighter, a glowing orange as he realises that he may finally be able to write properly. Dr Kyle shows Cary some exercises that could help integrate this reflex and gives him information on calligraphy lessons that the other crabs are doing. Cary's pincers start twitching with excitement. He can't wait to get started!

Is Chaotic Cary finally going to become a calm crab with clear writing?

Chapter Seven: Maximillian the Marine Iguana

Maximillian is Ollie's oddball friend. We all have that one friend that doesn't quite fit in our circle of friends. Maximillian, being a reptile, has a fierce expression that hides the fact that he's actually a gentle vegetarian and eats algae and seaweed. If you met Maxi, you would be so certain that he was going to eat you! Or at least take a chunk out of your leg!

Many believe that marine iguanas evolved from land dwelling iguanas of South America that drifted away on logs, landing on the Galapagos Islands. No one really knows how Maximillian travelled to Tasmania, though. Was he stowaway on a ship? Australia's quarantine officers would have a fit, with their very strict laws that protect our country ecologically. Was Maxi captured by pirates who sailed here? It definitely gives him a sense of mystery, and his presence often sends shivers down the spines of the other sea creatures.

Maxi's writing looks like scratches and scribbles on a rock. Ollie wonders whether it is because of his long and sharp claws. They look frightening, like they could create a lot of damage. Maxi's eyes cross when looking at a person, and his hand and eye movements are so jerky, it reminds Ollie of the zombie creatures that are written about in books. No wonder he is scary to everyone else.

Dr Brandon is brave enough to tackle Maximillian. He discovers that Maxi still has his asymmetrical tonic neck reflex. This reflex should have disappeared six months after birth. If it hasn't, then this could cause handwriting and eye tracking issues, making it harder to read. It also causes poor hand-eye coordination and creates issues when catching a ball or dancing!

Maxi's eyes pop out even further. "You mean I will be able to dance?" he whispers to Dr Brandon. "Even the samba?" Maxi's long tail swishes in the water in eager anticipation.

"What's the samba?" asks Ollie.

Kiki the Pink Seahorse, who has been bobbing amongst the kelp fronds, glides in closer.

"Yay, we can do the samba, Maxi. I can teach you," Kiki cries out.

"Ollie, it's just about the best dance ever but you need to be coordinated." Kiki bobs about, showing Ollie and Maxi some of her intricate moves.

Dr Brandon gives Maxi some exercises. Can you believe that the exercises are called the "lizard" and the "reverse lizard"?

Maxi is so excited that he signs up for some samba lessons with Kiki straightaway.

Chapter Eight: Gloria the Giant Clam

Dr Robert Melillo spots Gloria the Giant Clam sheltered under a rock shelf in the kelp forest. He is amazed at this discovery as giant clams generally live in the warmer waters of the South Pacific and Indian Oceans.

Ollie explains that Gloria was accidently washed overboard on a marine expedition as an itsy-bitsy tiny clam, and set up her home in that particular patch of the kelp forest. Clams only get one chance to set up their home. Once a clam fastens itself to a spot on the reef, it sits there for the rest of its life. It is just by pure luck that Gloria is now part of Ollie's gang.

Dr Robert is an amazing storyteller and a captivating lecturer. His students all over the world are enthralled during his lectures. In a hushed voice, he tells the group about the "man eater" myths of the giant clam. Legendary divers in the South Pacific claim that these giant clams lie in wait to trap unsuspecting swimmers and occasionally swallow them whole.

Ollie's eyes grow wide, and he gasps, "OH MY!"

Dr Rob reassures the gang and Gloria that there has, however, been no account of any humans killed by giant clams. Gloria has adductor muscles, or thigh muscles, that move WAY too slowly to take any swimmer unawares. Dr Kyle and Dr Brandon are very pleased by this.

On examining Gloria, Dr Rob finds that she has a retained rooting reflex. Gloria is known to stutter when she talks, so she often remains shy and retiring, avoiding playing with the gang. Ollie has often noticed that Gloria has a habit of biting her lips constantly or playing with her lips. She is also known to drool when she attempts to speak. It certainly doesn't help her win friends as the gang finds it a little gross, to be honest.

Dr Rob is super confident that after certain exercises, Gloria should be able to speak without stuttering or drooling. Dr Rob says to Ollie, "Ollie, are you ready for a very important assignment?"

"Sure," gurgles Ollie, puffing out with self-importance.

"I need you to help Gloria with the cat whiskers exercises."

"Cat whiskers! Will I need a cat? I have heard about these furry creatures that live on land but I have never actually seen one. How can I get one? How would a cat even travel down to the kelp forest?" Ollie replies, his mind racing and his response a jumble of words.

"No, that's ok, you don't actually need a cat," chuckles Dr Rob. "Ollie, all you need to do is draw cat whiskers towards Gloria's lips using your tentacles, which will help activate Gloria's rooting reflex. Do you know what cat whiskers look like?"

"Oh, of course I have seen a picture of a cat. I can definitely draw these," declares Ollie, his mind plotting on how he could use some pink coral to do so. He was actually planning to draw a cat on Gloria's shell. He really is a mischievous octopus!

Chapter Nine: Odyssey the Sea Lion

The lucky last to be checked is Odyssey the Sea Lion.

Just the other day, Ollie's mum was reading a huge book titled *The Odyssey*. Ollie was intrigued and had asked her whether it was a book about the sea lion that had just joined the colony. That's when he found out that *The Odyssey* was a book of ancient poems about a Greek hero called Odysseus, who was the king of a place called Ithaca, and his journey home after the Trojan War. Odyssey is a name that means wanderer, journey or crusade.

Ollie looks at the big grey sea lion doing loops and swoops in the kelp forest. He can't believe how well the name "Odyssey" suits his new friend. Whispers and rumours abounded when Odyssey first joined the community in the kelp forest a week ago. How did he get here? Did he hitch a ride? Was it on a lifeboat or hanging out on the back of a fast speedboat? Was he kidnapped and did he escape? The real answer is that Odyssey simply swam the 1000 kilometres to get here.

Did you know that sea lions are incredible creatures that can swim up to 50 kilometres an hour?

A few days ago, Odyssey had confided in Ollie his quest to discover answers to his quirks! Odyssey can never stay still, he is always on the move, squirming – like he had ants in the pants, as they say. His concentration skills are woeful, and he can't focus on one thing for any more than 5 minutes.

He tried, and tried, and tried so hard to fit in with his colony from Kangaroo Island.

Then there is his secret. In a really hushed voice and with a wave of embarrassment, he confided in Ollie that he almost always wets his bed! No matter what tricks his parents tried, he just couldn't help it. It made life unbearable. So when Odyssey heard about the Melillo party, he just had to swim all this way to find the answers to his problems. He is so lucky that his huge hairy whiskers proved to be a superb navigation system, better than any GPS in the world.

Despite his problems, Odyssey is a party animal at heart and loves to socialise. He has the most playful nature, and in the short time he has been in the kelp forest, Ollie's gang has come to adore him. His flippers give him such incredible agility that his tricks are superb. Being mainly a land creature, Odyssey has to hold his breath to visit Ollie and his gang so many metres underwater. His record for holding his breath is an amazing 25 minutes, a whole 5 minutes more than the average sea lion.

Although he has come such a far distance, Odyssey is overcome with shame and embarrassment. He simply can't find the courage to swim up to the doctors and voice his problems. With a heavy heart and running out of breath, Odyssey shoots up to the surface.

As the party is coming to a close, Ollie realises that Odyssey has not been examined and cannot be seen anywhere. Ollie asks Dr Brandon in a soft voice if there is any chance his friend could be helped. Dr Brandon listens carefully and nods his head.

"Ah, yes!" Dr Brandon exclaims. "It sounds like Odyssey has the retained spinal Galant reflex."

The spinal Galant reflex is designed to help during the birthing process. If retained it is demonstrated by the inability to sit still, poor concentration and bedwetting! Ollie begs Dr Brandon to examine Odyssey.

Ollie is excited that there may be a cure for Odyssey. This Melillo Method™ and integrating retained primitive reflexes is proving to be an elixir of hope for many of his friends. Ollie swishes around looking for his friend. He can see a big blob bobbing about, high above on the surface. Using a shiny oyster shell, Ollie reflects the light streaming down. The sharp glint of light hits Odyssey straight in the eye! Odyssey looks down below and can see Ollie signalling for him to dive down.

With a quick flick of those strong back flippers, Odyssey is beside Dr Brandon in a flash. After a few "oohs" and a final "aha", Dr Brandon turns to Odyssey and says, "As I expected, you do have a retained spinal Galant reflex!"

Dr Brandon then demonstrates the snow angel exercises Odyssey has to do. As Odyssey watches, he feels a funny quiver down his spine. He has found the answer he has been looking for! Sea lions are known as "angels of the sea", due to their front flippers looking like angel wings. This, like his name, was surely no simple coincidence.

Odyssey's whole body lights up in excitement and tingles. He realises that he has found the Nirvana of his spiritual wanderings. It was indeed the most magnificent day in discovering the Melillo Method™ and meeting with the handsome Dr Brandon.

The sunlight slowly fades and it is time for the three world famous Neuro Musketeers to return to their boat. It will be a while before these sea creatures meet them again.

Ollie feels so proud of himself that he had the courage to speak with Dr Rob. The Melillo Method™ and integrating primitive reflexes can really give Ollie and his friends truly magnificent brains.

Chapter Ten: Grand Finale

Six months after the Melillo party . . .

It is a crisp and fresh morning in New York. Central Park is awash in colour, with the leaves carpeting the ground in splashes of the brightest sunniest yellow to the deeper reds and purples, rustling and swirling at the slightest breeze. Dr Robert Melillo is super busy in his New York clinic. Janet, his amazing PA, comes bustling in during his first break of the day.

"Look at what has arrived!" she exclaims, presenting an envelope beautifully addressed with stunning calligraphy.

"Oh wow! It looks like an invitation to high tea with the Queen. Can you please read it?" Dr Rob replies.

"It is an invitation to a grand ball in the kelp forest of Tasmania, from Ollie and his gang. It is signed by Cary. I simply cannot believe that Chaotic Cary the Crab has written this. The penmanship is just so perfect and, based on your notes, he could barely scribble when you last saw him!"

"I was just dreaming of Australia!" murmurs Dr Rob.

"Quick, Janet!" Dr Rob cries out. "Book my tickets immediately."

At the same time, in different parts of the United States, Dr Kyle and Dr Brandon also receive the same invitation. With excitement and anticipation, they are on the phone to each other making plans. The time has come for another trip to Australia.

The day of the ball . . .

There is a buzz in the kelp forest. Everyone is so excited that they are making the grownups groan in despair. Ollie is darting in between the kelp blades as the Southern Oceanic Orchestra rehearses. When he can finally sit still, Ollie starts to practice with his juggling balls, but he is just too excited and he keeps dropping them.

Cries of "Ollie!" echo in the forest, as yet another sea creature trips over his juggling balls.

If only you could be there. Your spine would be tingling, and you would feel the vibrations of anticipation. Have you ever been so excited that you could not sit still or sleep?

As the sun sets, the crashing waves produce streams of effervescent bubbles which spiral down to the ocean floor, creating curtains of sparkling diamonds. It adds to the atmosphere for the ball and looks like a work of art. Nature is truly beautiful.

Suddenly, the shadows of the three divers are noted. Nearly everyone gasps in delight. The show is about to begin.

Blacktip reef sharks glide from the shadows to greet Dr Rob, Dr Kyle and Dr Brandon. They are handed a program written once again in beautiful calligraphy by Chaotic Cary the Crab, and are directed to their seats.

The show is about to begin.

As the Southern Oceanic Orchestra begins playing, the kelp curtains start to pull open, and the spotlight is on Daisy the Dolphin wearing an amazing sparkling outfit. The lights reflect off her gown, creating a disco ball of shimmering light through the crowds.

Daisy begins the show by reading a warm welcome speech. Her voice is loud and clear, and there is no stumbling on her words or hesitation. She belongs on stage.

"Oh?" exclaims Dr Rob. "Is this the same Daisy? To be reading as well as she does, her left brain has built new networks and become truly magnificent."

The first act is Stormy the Starfish telling funny jokes, all from memory. She is beaming and glowing, looking so friendly. Could this possibly be the same Stormy? Should we be renaming her Smiley the Starfish? She is absolutely dazzling on stage, remembering all her jokes without any trouble. She makes the whole audience laugh so hard, some sea creatures even fall off their seats!

The orchestra strikes up some lively samba music that has everyone dancing in their seats. Low and behold, it is Maximillian the Marine Iguana doing an amazing samba dance with one of the blacktip reef sharks. They just glide on stage, and Kiki the Pink Seahorse can be seen bobbing up and down near the kelp curtains. She is so proud of Maxi, as he not only worked hard at dance lessons, but he completed all the lizard exercises twice a day.

Ollie is the closing act. He manages to find all his juggling balls and performs incredibly well. He does not drop a single ball, even with the trickier moves. His mum is beaming in her seat as Ollie is in his element and performing to his true potential. It has been a challenging journey, and she is super proud of what he has achieved, with more than a few tears in her eyes. Ollie's dream of becoming a famous juggler of the Seven Seas is within his reach. It is so important to have a grand dream, and to never ever QUIT! Anything is possible with hope.

Dr Robert Melillo's face is beaming with pride. It makes his life's work so worthwhile helping these sea creatures, as he does with children all over the world, to reach their true potential. Dr Rob, Dr Kyle and Dr Brandon – the three Neuro Musketeers – all leap from their seats to give a standing ovation.

After the show, Sally the Shrimp rushes over to show them her trophy from the athletics carnival. Silly Sally no longer has that weird running style.

Ollie proceeds to share Odyssey the Sea Lion's journey. Odyssey returned to South Australia as he had found the elixir of his quest, the Melillo Method™. He no longer wets the bed! While Ollie is talking, Dr Rob glances over to where Gloria the Giant Clam lives. He has to stifle a giggle, as there on her shell is the bright pink cat that Ollie had painted. Ollie may have integrated his primitive reflexes, but his cheekiness and personality will always be the same.

As the divers are getting ready to leave, looking closely, there is a glint of tears in their eyes. The Melillo Method™ is their why, and their life's work.

"Ollie, your brain is truly magnificent!" exclaims Dr Rob as they reach the surface.

Integrating Primitive Reflexes Exercises

If you need some direction in finding out which retained reflexes are still active in your child, Dr Robert Melillo's book *Disconnected Kids* is a great guide. For a more visual approach, please check out www.ollietheoctopus.com.au, where a self-guided video course is available to purchase.

The following exercises are suitable for ages 4 and up.

Disclaimer

The exercises in this book are intended to be conducted under the supervision of an adult and used only in conjunction with advice received from a qualified professional. The exercises do not replace therapeutic evaluation of a child's development, and use of the retained reflexes integration should not occur without supervision from a qualified health care practitioner. Any liability arising from unauthorised and/or unsupervised use of these techniques is excluded to the maximum extent permissible.

Babinski Reflex

The Babinski reflex is present at birth and starts to fade at one year. It helps initiate exercising the baby's feet. This reflex assists the baby to crawl by pushing the toes into the floor to help push off in crawling, to create forward movement. A positive Babinski is when the big toe curls back in extension and the little toes flare. A positive Planter is when the toes curl forward. For a integrated Babinksi, we should see no reaction.

A retained Babinski reflex may lead to:
- delays in learning to walk
- poor balance
- tripping and falling

Integration Exercise

- Using the blunt end of a pen or toothbrush, in one motion gently stroke up the outside of the bottom of the child's foot towards their little toe, then along the base of the toes towards their big toe.
- Do this 5 times for each foot, twice a day.

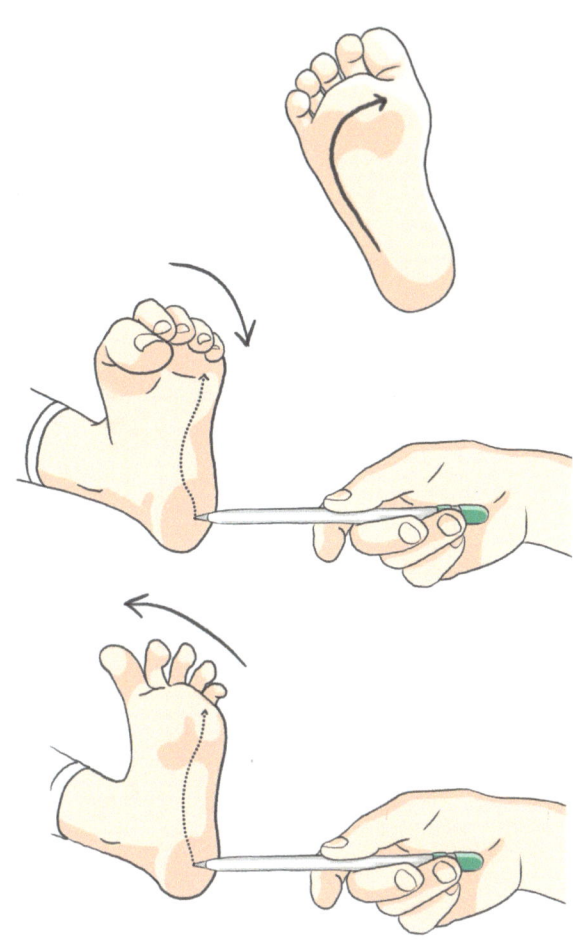

Startle Reflex

The infant startle reflex is also known as the Moro reflex. When a baby is startled by a loud noise or sudden movement, they will suddenly extend their limbs outward and arch their back, before drawing their limbs back toward and in front of their body. The baby might also gasp or cry.

A retained startle reflex may lead to:
- hypersensitivity and overreaction to sudden noise, movement, or light
- mood swings with aggressive outbursts
- dislike of change or anything new
- feelings of constant anxiety

Integration Exercise: Starfish

- While sitting, have the child extend their arms and legs open like a starfish, with their head tilted slightly back as they breathe in.
- As they breathe out, get them to slowly lower their head toward their chest while they cross their legs and arms, with the right leg and right arm on top. Their arms should be crossed over their chest like an "X".
- On their next breath in, get them to do the starfish, then on the breath out, cross their arms and legs, this time with the left arm and left leg on top.
- Do this 5 times for each side, twice a day.

" Starfish "

Right on top

" Starfish "

Left on top

Rooting Reflex

The first primitive reflexes a baby adapts at birth are the rooting and sucking reflexes. The rooting reflex is triggered when the skin around a baby's mouth is stimulated by touch, causing them to open their mouth and turn towards the stimulus. This reflex helps a baby find a source of food, either a breast or a bottle, and start feeding successfully.

A retained rooting reflex may lead to:
- speech issues
- involuntary tongue or mouth movements when writing or drawing
- chewing or biting lips constantly

Integration Exercise

- Lightly stroke the child's face horizontally inward from the ear toward the lips 3 times on each side. Make sure you touch the corner of the lips.
- Lower the starting point by about ½ inch each time.
- Use a make-up brush as if you are painting cat whiskers, or your fingers if the child is super sensitive.
- Do this exercise twice a day.

Palmer Reflex

From the moment of birth, an infant will grasp your finger and hang on for dear life when you stroke the palm of their hand. This is normal for the first few months of life. However, if it does not integrate, it will impact individual finger movements.

A retained palmer reflex may lead to:
- poor fine motor skills
- inappropriate, immature pencil grip
- poor or messy handwriting

Integration Exercise

- Have the child hold a small squishy ball in their hands.
- Get them to squish the ball with all their fingers and thumb in a slow controlled motion.
- Get them to squish the ball between their thumb and each finger separately.
- Do this 5 times for each hand, twice a day.

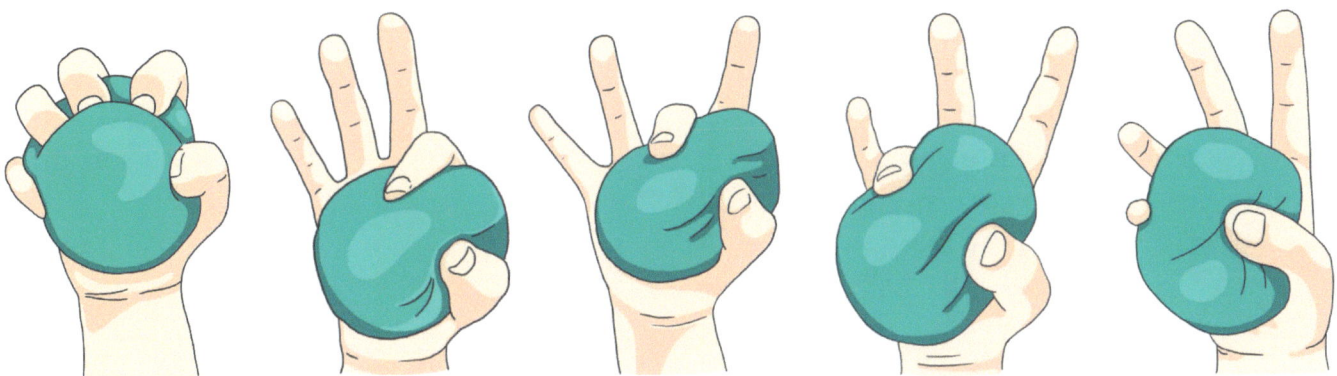

Asymmetrical Tonic Neck Reflex (ATNR)

This reflex is believed to be important for a baby's movement through the birth canal. It also helps a baby roll over and to start to crawl.

A retained ATNR reflex may lead to:
- poor handwriting
- difficulty reading and tracking, missing parts of the lines when reading
- poor hand-eye coordination, causing difficulties with sports and other activities

Integration Exercise – Lizard and Reverse Lizard

Lizard
- Have the child lie face-down on the floor, with their right knee bent up at a 90-degree angle and their right elbow bent so that their right hand is level with their face. Their left arm and leg should be straight beside their body. Have the child turn their head to the right to face their hand.
- Next, have the child switch positions to the other side, so their head is turned to the left, their left knee is bent at a 90-degree angle, and their left elbow is bent with their hand level with their head.
- The child should bring their right arm and leg straight down at the same time as they bring their left arm and leg up.
- Do this 5-6 times, twice a day.

Reverse Lizard

The movements for the reverse lizard are the same movements as the lizard, except the child's head should turn *away* from their hand.

- Have the child lie face-down on the floor, with their right knee bent up at a 90-degree angle and their right elbow bent so that their right hand is level with their face. Their left arm and leg should be straight beside their body. Have the child turn their head to the left to face away from their hand.
- Next, have the child switch positions to the other side, so their head is turned to the right, their left knee is bent at a 90-degree angle, and their left elbow is bent with their hand level with their head.
- The child should bring their right arm and leg straight down at the same time as they bring their left arm and leg up.
- Do this 5-6 times, twice a day.

Spinal Galant Reflex

This is the reflex that helps a baby move through the birth canal. It also helps a baby roll over.

A retained spinal Galant reflex could lead to:
- inability to sit still or remain silent
- poor concentration
- continued bed wetting beyond the age of 5 years

Integration Exercise – Snow Angel

- With the child lying on their back, have them raise their straight arms above their head in slow controlled movements.
- While doing this, have them spread their legs outwards at the same time, as if they are creating snow angels.
- Then they should slowly lower their arms down to their side at the same time as they bring their legs together.
- Do this 10 times, twice a day.

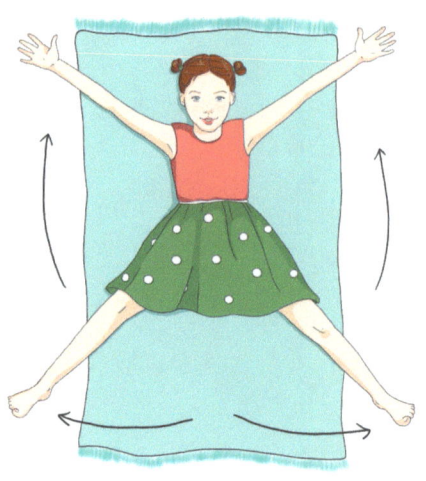
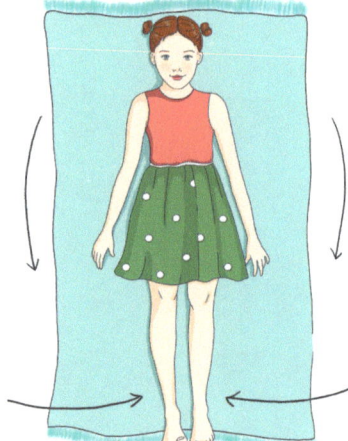

DR ROBERT MELILLO (USA) is a respected specialist in developmental functional neurology, brain imbalances, hemispheric integration, and the diagnosis and correction of most neurobehavioural disorders and learning disabilities in the United States.

His clinical experience, research, and success with patients in his private practice led Dr Melillo to create the Brain Balance Achievement Centres in 2006. There are now over 100 centres across the USA.

Dr Melillo is a prolific researcher and author. In 2004, he published *Neurobehavioral Disorders of Childhood: An Evolutionary Perspective*, a working-theory textbook on developmental disabilities. He has published a number of other books on childhood neurobehavioural disorders, including the best-selling *Disconnected Kids*, which has since been translated into eight languages. Dr Melillo has also published numerous scientific papers, and contributed chapters to textbooks on topics such as dyslexia, attention, and frontal lobe development.

Dr Melillo is an adjunct professor at the National University of Health Sciences and is a senior research fellow with the National Institute for Brain and Rehabilitation Sciences. He holds a master's degree in clinical rehabiltation neuropsychology, a doctorate in chiropractic, and he is completing a PhD in cognitive neuroscience. He is also the co-founder and past president of the International Association of Functional Neurology and Rehabilitation.

Dr Melillo also serves on the advisory board for Grammy-award-winning musician Zac Brown's inclusive camp, Camp Southern Ground.

Dr Melillo and his wife, Carolyn, are also the creators of the web series *Disconnected Kids, Reconnected Families*, a documentary-style series helping families face and overcome childhood neurobehavioural issues.

Learn more about Dr Melillo and his work at www.drrobertmelillo.com, or follow him on Instagram, @drrobertmelillo and Facebook, at facebook.com/drrobertmelillo.

GENEVIEVE DHARAMARAJ is an Australian allied healthcare practitioner with over 25 years' experience. She holds a bachelor's degree in science, a master's degree in chiropractic, and a master's degree in paediatric chiropractic. She has been awarded a Fellowship in Childhood Neurodevelopment Disorders from the International Board of Functional Neurology.

Noticing a spike in children experiencing learning and behavioural difficulties, Gen began to explore and study functional neurological concepts not normally associated with the field she was currently in.

Dr Robert Melillo's work inspired Gen to study and travel to Europe for face-to-face conferences. She was lucky to shadow Dr Rob in Bulgaria where he saw children with severe autism. This inspired her to open a separate business for functional neurology, launching Nurturing Brain Potential – the first therapeutic clinic in Australia to utilise the work of Dr Melillo. Nurturing Brain Potential is the result of lifelong learning, passion and determination to help children with difficulties rise to meet their potential.

When Gen isn't working, she enjoys training for triathlons, spending time with her family, or shopping in her favourite precincts with her friends.

Learn more about Genevieve Dharamaraj and Nurturing Brain Potential at www.nurturingbrainpotential.com.au, or on Instagram, @nurturingbrainpotential.

 **DR KYLE DAIGLE (USA)** is a chiropractor, business owner and inventor. He is the owner of Ultimate Performance Chiro & Rehab in Lake Chares, where he helps numerous collegiate and professional athletes to achieve their maximum performance through his state-of-the-art treatment as well as nutritional protocols. He attended Parker College of Chiropractic (now Parker University) in Dallas, where he studied functional neurology and functional medicine and was the president of the Nutrition Club. He has been awarded a Fellowship in Childhood Neurodevelopmental Disorders from the International Board of Functional Neurology.

Dr Daigle is currently the Chief Medical Officer for SNA Technologies, where he co-developed the non-invasive, non-pharmacological therapy platform Neurosage. He is a managing partner for BrainChat, an online neurological rehabilitation educational platform for doctors and therapists, and is a managing partner for Neuro Solution, a company bringing the power of laser and light therapy to the forefront of medical treatment. Dr Daigle also has a consulting company, LegendaryDC Consulting, where he helps clinicians with practice and case management.

In 2018, Dr Daigle was awarded the International Association of Functional Neurology and Rehabilitation (IAFNR) Humanitarian Award, and in 2019 received the Lifetime Achievement Award. He is also the author of the book, *What If You Knew? A Revolutionary Approach to Regaining Your Health and Life*.

Dr Daigle lives with his wife and two children.

Learn more about Dr Kyle Daigle at www.snabiotech.com, or connect with him on Instagram, @dr.kyledaigledc.

DR BRANDON CRAWFORD (USA) has been awarded a Fellowship in Childhood Neurodevelopmental Disorders from the International Board of Functional Neurology.

He attended Parker College of Chiropractic (now Parker University) in Dallas, where he earned a PhD in chiropractic. Dr Crawford is known for working in the field of photobiomodulation, specifically how to apply laser and light therapy to the brain and nervous system, and lectures globally on these topics.

Dr Crawford owns a very active clinical practice in Cedar Park, Texas, where he works with patients from around the world. Dr Crawford is co-founder of the company Neuro Solution, which he founded to spread the modality of laser and light therapy across the globe. Dr Crawford serves on advisory boards for SNA Technologies, maker of the Neurosage software, and for BrainTap. Dr Crawford is also managing partner in LegendaryDC Consulting, a consulting firm for practitioners interested in implementing innovative methods into their practice and growing their business.

Dr Crawford is passionate about traveling the world, and spending time with his wife and their two sons.

Learn more about Dr Crawford at www.neuro-solution.com, or on Instagram, @bcrawforddc.

 Sydney-based artist and illustrator **KAT SMIRNOFF** has had a fascination with painting and creating art from an early age. Growing up in the Lithuanian countryside, she developed a deep love for the outdoors and nature; which then became the biggest inspiration for her work. Kat's connection with the natural world, plants and animals is represented in her vibrant, colourful and detailed designs, illustrations and murals.

In 2017, she created Kat's Mural Art. Since then, she has been successfully applying her art on the walls of numerous childcare centres, hospitals, clinics, restaurants and cafés, as well as private residences in Brisbane and Sydney.

Kat's preferred art medium is watercolour and acrylic. More recently she has also developed a passion for digital painting, a skill that has been applied to *Ollie the Octopus and His Magnificent Brain*™.

Learn more about Kat and her work at www.katsmuralart.com. You can also connect with Kat on Facebook at facebook.com/kasmuralart, or Instagram, @katsmuralart.

CPSIA information can be obtained
at www.ICGtesting.com
Printed in the USA
LVHW071313211021
701064LV00006B/51